John Hoyt Lockwood

A Sermon Commemorative of the Two-Hundredth Anniversary of the First Congregational Church of Westfield, Mass.

John Hoyt Lockwood

A Sermon Commemorative of the Two-Hundredth Anniversary of the First Congregational Church of Westfield, Mass.

ISBN/EAN: 9783337087647

Printed in Europe, USA, Canada, Australia, Japan

Cover: Foto ©ninafisch / pixelio.de

More available books at **www.hansebooks.com**

A SERMON

COMMEMORATIVE OF THE

Two-Hundredth Anniversary

OF THE

First Congregational Church

OF

WESTFIELD, MASS.,

DELIVERED BY THE PASTOR,

Rev. JOHN H. LOCKWOOD,

SUNDAY, OCTOBER 5, 1879,

To which an Appendix is added.

PUBLISHED BY REQUEST.

WESTFIELD, MASS.:
CLARK & STORY, PRINTERS.
1879.

1415155

Copy of Correspondence.

Westfield, October 6, 1879.

Rev. J. H. Lockwood,—*Dear Sir:*—We, on behalf of the Society of the First Congregational Church of Westfield, respectfully request of you a copy of your Bi-Centennial Historical Sermon for publication.

HENRY W. BATES,
JUNIUS A. TALMADGE,
LYMAN M. SMITH,
} *Prudential Committee.*

Westfield, October 6, 1879.

Messrs. HENRY W. BATES, JUNIUS A. TALMADGE, and LYMAN M. SMITH,—*Gentlemen:*—Since the Bi-Centennial Historical Sermon, delivered yesterday in the First Church, is, in your estimation, worthy of publication in a permanent form, I cheerfully place it at your disposal, with such additions as seem worthy of preservation with it; but which, incorporated into it, would have made it too long for delivery at a single Sabbath service.

Respectfully Yours,

JOHN H. LOCKWOOD.

PREFATORY NOTE.

Many difficulties beset the preparation of such a sketch as is here attempted. The task has been not simply to collect annals of the old church, and not simply to prepare an address upon it; but it includes both, and more besides. As it would probably become a document of some historical value to future generations, it was important to include in it many interesting reminiscences with exact dates, and as it was to be delivered on the occasion of a regular church service, it needed to be restricted in extent and partake somewhat of the character of a sermon. Many items of interest to antiquarians, or to those whose families have lived here for many generations, and many others that are simply amusing and curious, were therefore excluded as outside the scope of the task. Some of them are accorded a place in the Appendix, which I would be glad to enlarge indefinitely were it not for the fear that it might thereby make too voluminous what is intended to be merely a brief sketch, and not an exhaustive treatise. It is also to be remembered that the discourse was prepared with the Town Bi-Centennial volume before me, in which are many deeply interesting facts relating to the early days of the town and the church, not only in the address, but also in the letters from former residents and reminiscences in the appendix, some of which would be included here were they not preserved there in permanent form. A few copies of that inval-

nable volume remain unsold, and may be secured at the news-
room of Mr. W. P. Meacham.

The many persons who have kindly proffered assistance, without which this task would have been utterly hopeless to one who
has been a resident of the town only six months, will please accept thanks therefor. Among them special mention should be
made of Mr. Henry Holland, who having made a special study
of local antiquities, has been of great service in determining
sites of historic interest, and in giving other valuable information ;
and Mr. David M. Chace, the Town Clerk, who has afforded the
fullest facilities for examining the town records.

JOHN H. LOCKWOOD.

SERMON.

I. Kings, viii., 57.—The Lord our God be with us as he was with our fathers.

This year marks a noteworthy epoch in the history of our church. Time has rolled on with steady flow till two hundred years have passed since it was organized by a handful of faithful disciples. The future for which they provided, so much of which is now past with its checkered record of human experience, was hidden from sight, but they laid foundations in faith and others have builded thereupon. Taking twenty years as the measure of a generation, this church has been the earthly home of ten generations of believers, where they have heard the everlasting gospel; where they have raised to the throne of grace praises and supplications; where they have brought sacrifices of themselves and their possessions. In this new world, whose remotest history is so recent, the churches that have passed through the vicissitudes of two centuries are comparatively few.

Among those of our own order, which are naturally the oldest in New England, there are forty-seven that exceed this church in age, of which one is in York, Me., organized in 1672, seventeen are in Connecticut, and twenty-nine are in Massachusetts. Several of them are but a few years older, and there are several also but a few years younger. No surer criterion of the rapidity with which the fathers entered into possession of this land of Canaan can be found than that suggested by the dates of the organization of the first churches of New England. In recognition of their Christian heroism, as well as God's long-continued blessing upon their labors, we should commemorate this remarkable anniversary. The formal exercises of organization occurred

August 27th, 1679 ; and, though the corresponding date of this year is passed, yet for the sake of convenience a formal observance of the occasion has been delayed till now.

The task of preparing a brief and interesting sketch of the church's history is beset by some difficulties besides those common to all historians. The available materials are very limited ; many of them have been carefully investigated and ably displayed by different persons within a few years, and are therefore somewhat familiar to most of those who are interested in the church ; and in a stable and conservative community like this, local traditions are carefully perpetuated. Families that have lived here for many generations naturally gather up facts relating to their ancestors for their own gratification, and to impart in turn to their children. Many family trees planted here in the early days of the settlement still flourish like monarchs of the forest. But though I may not discover in the records of the past many facts unfamiliar to those who were privileged to hear the carefully-prepared sketch of the town's history incorporated into the address of a member of this congregation, Hon. William G. Bates, delivered ten years ago when its bi-centennial was celebrated ; or to those who listened before that time to the various historical sermons of my predecessor, Rev. Dr. Emerson Davis, whose memory is still so sweetly fragrant wherever he was known ; yet it may be pleasant even to them to be stirred up by way of remembrance. Many strangers have also come among us within the last decade, and many children have matured from infancy to capacity to understand and enjoy stories of the past. While studying all original sources of information available, I shall use, freely and gratefully, the results of those who have preceded me in the field to be traversed at this time, hoping, not to excel them, but only to follow closely in their footsteps, and perhaps to beat two paths into one that may be more easily traversed by others who shall follow. In order that no available material might be lost I have carefully searched anew the town and church records from the beginning, and shall quote from them freely, believing that their quaint language and plain statements are more interesting than they would be if clothed in modern dress, and that they may never again be annotated. It has been so interesting to me to study the course of events making up our church history, as recorded in original documents, yellow with age and often in almost illegible chirography, though involving weeks of patient study, that I desire to share the pleasure, as far as possible, by giving you a literal transcript of what may never fall under your eyes in original form. The task in hand differs in scope from that of Mr. Bates; in extent from that of Dr. Davis already referred to;—the former having prepared a sketch of the town, and the latter in various published documents, of which I have copies, delineating briefer periods;.but now my effort is to trace the history and affairs of this church for two centuries. This attempt includes within its scope matters relating to the origin, growth and changes of the church, and facts of importance in the lives of its officers and members. Until a comparatively recent period the church has been so fully identified with the town that the records of the latter contain much relating to the former,—all the secular affairs of the church having been attended to at town meetings, as part of their prescribed business, where it was decided even to call every minister who preceded the Rev. Dr. Davis, settled in 1836.

The first reference in the town records to ecclesiastical affairs bears date of March 19, 1666, when a lot of twelve acres was set apart for the minister, " if he should like it ;" intimating that the act was done in anticipation of his arrival. According to the detailed account of Mr. Taylor of the origin of this church, no one came to occupy the land till a little later. He says:

" Westfield, then Warronnokee, coming to be an English plantation, had at first Mr. John Holyoake, son to that Godly Capt. Elizur Holyoake of Springfield, to dispense ye word of life amongst them, An° D^{mi}, 1667, about half a year ; but in ye beginning of winter following, he as finding y^r ministry of the word too heavie for him desisted ; from which time till ye beginning of winter 1668 they had no minister."

In August, 1668, the town acted as follows, after deciding to allow a minister the sum of £40 a year, to be derived by taxes on the lands :

" It is voted that we look at ourselves as free & at liberty to seek out according as God shall guide us for a minister to carry on the work of Christ here."

Their first laborer in the spiritual vineyard must have given satisfaction, for they voted " that George Phelps & James Cornish shall go to Springfield to trade with Mr. Hollyoke &
2

receive his answer." The spirit of thrift and prudence seems by the term thus used to have pervaded thus early even church business. Mr. Holyoke not consenting, it was voted soon afterward " that Capt. Cook shall go into the Bay to procure a minister, such a one as he shall be advised to by the elders in or about the bay if the Committee at Springfield do approve of our acts herein." He was ordered to take his journey "so soon as to be in the bay the .first Sabbath in October," about a week later. James Cornish was to go the next day to Springfield to consult the committee under whose auspices the town was settled, " & to speak to Capt. Pynchon & desire him to promote the design in the bay." Proof of the interest taken by these neighbors in the efforts of the infant colony to procure a minister is shown by the fact that during the next month, October, 1668, a farther grant of land to Westfield was made on condition that a minister should be procured within two years. There is no account of the result of the errand to the Bay, but the Rev. Moses Fisk, son of a minister of the church at Chelmsford, was gotten there, probably by Capt. Cook, who served the people three years, and then left them. They then tried to get the Rev. Mr. Adams of Dedham, and " finding ye said Mr. Adams not as yet movable from ye collidge," Mr. Taylor says:

" Their messenger was advised to myself (ye meanest of those that labour in Christ's vineyard) who upon advice did adventure to go with him home, and upon ye Lord's day following, being ye 3d of ye 10^m An° D^mi 1672, preached my first sermon amongst them from Matt. 3 : 2,—' Repent ye, for the kingdom of heaven is at hand.' "

He did not determine for some time to stay ; but, there being a prospect of organizing a church, he began to incline to settle with the people, and after serving them two years, he says : " We set up conference meetings at wch I went over all the Heads of Divinity unto ye means of ye application of Redemption before we did enter the church state." Their plans were delayed by the desolations and distractions of King Philip's war, which nearly destroyed the settlements at this end of the province. Two houses and barns were burned here, and several men were killed. The terror of the inhabitants was so great that several moved away, among them four of the nine church members of the place ; and the record says pathetically : " A sore temptation was thrust in upon us by the Adversary that seemed to threaten the overthrow of all proceedings unto a chh state by those by whom that interest was before most apparently devolved." But in the spring of 1679 they decided to call a council, to convene in August.* Five years before this, in 1674, Mr. Taylor married Elizabeth Fitch, daughter of the first clergyman of Norwich, Ct., a " highly educated & accomplished lady." One of his letters preliminary to that event, copied from the original among the archives of the Connecticut Historical Society, may be found in the appendix of the Town Bi-Centennial volume.† The provision for his support, even before his formal settlement, seems to have been generous. He received from £60 to £80 in those early years, besides large tracts of land. In addition to which the town voted in 1678 :

" That Lieut. Mosely & Isaac Phelps they are to take care about Mr. Taylor's hay & corn in hay time and harvest for the gathering of it in and the town are to spin Mrs. Taylor a day's work apiece in haytime & harvest & they are to have a day or two to said warning."

The account of the Council·is so quaintly and strikingly told that I shall quote Mr. Taylor's language quite extensively. Five churches were invited by letters missive. He proceeds : " These then being sent our work came on apace, for temptations having attended our work one time after time before, I for my part was unhearted until now to prepare, and therefore now I had both hands full & must go down into the hay before the time. Wherefore having often in private sought God together in order unto this matter now upon the 20th day of August, that day fo'night unto the day of assemblage we set apart for a fast to be kept by our whole town in order to yᵉ great work of yᵉ day of imbodying. on which day I preached from that 1 Kin. 8 : 57— ' yᵉ Lord our God be with us as he was with our fathers ; ' "—words I have myself chosen as not inappropriate for our consideration to-day. He showed from it that parents, when about to erect God's ordinances, ought to pray hard to God to be with them, and adds : " And as for the duty of prayer two of the brethren did help carry it on." In those early times it seems to have

*See Appendix A.
†See Appendix C.

been admissible for laymen to take part in the public service, at least on a Fast Day.

Of the five churches invited to the Council, four were represented. The church at Norwich did not respond; that at Windsor sent delegates, its pastor being detained at home by a domestic emergency. The three ministers who came were Rev. Peletiah Glover of Springfield, or "Cousin Glover," as Mr. Taylor calls him; with whom came also "ye worshipful Maj: John Pynchon," Rev. John Russel of Hadley, and the Rev. Solomon Stoddard of Northampton, who afterward became a leader among the advocates of the "half-way covenant." The members of the Council arrived on the evening preceding the day appointed, and began at once to examine into the affairs engaging them, and were greatly disturbed by discovering two serious obstacles in the way of accomplishing what the brethren desired. One was that Mr. Taylor, upon whom, as the candidate, devolved the delivery of the ordination sermon, proposed to preach in the afternoon, instead of beginning the work of the day with it. The other and more serious one was, that the statement of doctrine on which the church was to be recognized consisted only of the Confession of Faith of the Westminster Assembly and the Cambridge Platform, which the Council deemed insufficient; this, however, was also in some way removed. We can but note a contrast between the prudence of that time and the laxity of the present, when churches are admitted to Congregational fellowship simply offering the Bible to be interpreted by a majority vote of its members at any time. In his statement before the Council, Mr. Taylor reviewed the history of the enterprise, presented letters of dismissal of those who were to be organized from their respective churches, and a formal commission to the christian people of Westfield in general, and seven men named in particular, to enter into a church state, signed by John Leverett, Governor, and six assistants.*

I cannot forbear quoting at some length Mr. Taylor's account of the concluding transactions of that ancient Council:

"After the confession of our faith was made we were called out to give some account of the workings of the Spirit upon our hearts that might be as a foundation for the charity of God's

---

*See Appendix B.

people to act upon in order to y⁰ approval of us in their souls as suitable matter for such a structure in hand. An account of which, so far as time would admit, was then personally given in these relations (here abbreviated) following, y⁰ which had at least some been read (and doubtless it would have been to more edification) had not y⁰ elders and messengers of Northampton and Hadley drove on to y⁰ contrary."

Then follow his and the Relations of the other six, written out at great length, being extravagant delineations of their conversion and subsequent experience. The sermon he delivered is copied out in full, making twelve pages folio of microscopic writing, which must have required at least three hours to preach it. This was before the days of sermonettes fifteen minutes long, which make some men popular. The sermon being ended, "y⁰ Moderator stood up & gave a brief account of what was done and propounded y⁰ brethren to y⁰ Elders and Messengers for their approbation unto their proceeding if they desired further satisfaction in y⁰ matter or judged anything yet further to be attended to in this case before the covenant was entered into, they were desired to manifest the same ; if otherwise let their silence manifest it. Whereupon nothing appearing y⁰ Moderator called us forth to enter covenant, which being done in y⁰ words of y⁰ covenant by and by recited he pronounced us a church of Christ orderly gathered according to y⁰ rules of Christ in y⁰ gospell." Mr. Stoddard gave the right hand of fellowship to the church. " This being done the Moderator demanded of y⁰ church whom they chose their officer and into what office. Whereupon y⁰ brethren of the church laid my unworthy self under a call unto y⁰ office of Pastor unto them." Rev. Messrs. Russel, Glover and Stoddard, with Samuel Loomis, one of the brethren of the church, laid on hands. " Mr. Russel prayed before ordination, Mr. Glover ordained, and Mr. Stoddard ended the work with prayer."

The church covenant into which the original seven members entered, is long, explicit, and solemn, and in the old church record book is signed in large letters by Edward Taylor, John Maudesly, Samuel Loomis, Josiah Dewy, John Root, Isaac Phelps, and John Ingerson (now Ingersoll). The common number of seven foundation-men was soon increased by one, as we learn from the following explanation :

" Brother Th Gun being nominated for a foundation man desired to be omitted and was admitted ye 21 ye 7 m without Relation, in that he was so much decayed by age that it would be a hard thing to gather it, and he was a man of approved piety and was recommended to us by Windsor church."

The method of receiving subsequent members was to consider them in conference meeting, then propound them "in ye Assembly that if any can give in any just ground against their Behaviour they have liberty." They were then voted on at a meeting preparatory to the Lord's Supper. After giving "an account of some of those experiences of God's work upon their hearts, ye w^h if they thro fearfulness and bashfulness do desire ye same may be read, ye chh complying to their desires therein the same as also it is on ye admitting of Women." After an affirmative vote the following covenant was read :

" We here in obedience unto Almighty God, in Christ receiving members into full communion in this chh of Christ amongst us and admitting you unto all Gospell privileges therein, according unto y^r several capacities thereunto, Do promise solemnly in ye presence of God to perform unto you as unto ourselves all those mutuall Duties of helpfulness unto wch we have mutually obliged ourselves, and do pronounce you Members of this chh of Christ orderly admitted."

The infant church thus constituted had no other officer than the pastor for many years. The account says : "No ruling elder nor Deacon was elected, only Brother Loomis was desired to look after the preparing wine and bread and to furnish ye Lord's table." He was afterward elected Deacon, but hesitating about accepting the office and waiting for the election of a colleague, he died without being ordained. It was not until 1692 that Josiah Dewey and Nathanael Weller were ordained the first of a long line of holy men who have served in that capacity ; so that the church was for thirteen years in that anomalous condition, having no officer but the pastor.

Where the people met for service during the early years is matter of conjecture, as no record that I can find refers to it. The exact time of the erection of the first meeting-house is also uncertain, the votes respecting it not being dated in the town records ; but it was probably about the time of organization. The first vote is as follows :

" That the town will go on with building a meeting house with all convenient speed as may be, the dimentions are as follows : About 36 feet square and for form like Hatfield meeting house, as the comitey chosen shall advise and agree."

The next, and only other recorded vote respecting it, is strangely muddled, but indicates that there had been some difficulty regarding the site, and that " after debating in the town, came to vote of the town to lott that the friend one of God should determine it, and after solemn looking of God the lots were drawn the lot came forth for the place before goodman Phelps or Goodman Gunns if Mr. Taylor se cause." The town voted to build " gallereys on each side of yᵉ meeting house" May 10th, 1703, indicating that the congregation was too large for the building. In those primitive times strict order was enforced by duly constituted authority, as is indicated by a town vote in 1689 :

" Walter Lee, Samuel Fowler and the Sergeant of the guard are appointed to take care of children on the Sabbath to see that they atend and keep their places both before and in the time of exercise."

As the town increased in population the church building, even with the " gallereys," became too small to accommodate the worshipers, and in 1717 the first recorded action was taken respecting a new house of- worship. Twice during the next year the subject came up again before the town for consideration, and November 17, 1719, " the town took into consideration the necessity that we are in to put ourselves into some way to find out a place to set and to build a new meeting house." In order to secure a peaceable settlement of difficulties about the site, they decided to leave the matter to arbitration, and a committee from Springfield was invited to decide it, consisting of Dea. John Munn, Lieut. John Merick and Benjamin Lennard, who soon afterward presented a characteristic report : " Gentlemen— seeing God in his providence hath called us according to your desire " (an instance of *vox populi, vox dei,*) " to consider your surcomstances and where may be yᵉ convenientest place for you to set your meeting house our result is on the northwest corner of Cap'n Maudesleys lot by the meadow gate." There being dissatisfaction, however, with this decision, it was voted to leave the matter with Cap'n Samuel Partridge, and abide by the result

he should reach. His report must have been formal and explicit
enough to satisfy the most exacting:

" Whereas the town of Westfield at a legal town meeting on
yᵉ 21 day of this instant December 1719 past an act in said
meeting they being at a difficulty in concluding the place to set
their new meeting house at and voated to leave the full desition
of that matter unto me undersigned upon which I together with
Cap'n John Ashley and Lieutenant Abijah Dewey went up to
yᵉ place of the cyder press their standing which I judged too fur
toward the West end of yᵉ town for conveniency of the peoples
meeting at yᵉ present allso I vewed yᵉ norwest corner of Deacon
Root desceased his lot I judged that place too near yᵉ dwelling
houses against and as to Mr Gunns paster and yᵉ lot where old
John Sacket lived too much to the South end of the town and
yᵉ old meeting house much more I allso vewed Cap'n Maudesleys
paster on yᵉ south side of the way and that I judge will be too
near Cap'n Roots barn therefore having maturely vewed the
knowl on Cap'n Maudesleys lot on the north side of yᵉ way
behind his housing I hereby determine to bee the place for erect-
ing and setting up the new meeting house this I deliver as my
positive opinion upon the premises.   SAMUELL PARTRIDGE."

The form of the new building is somewhat more fully suggested than that of the old one. It was to be built " barn fation
with a bell coney upon the middle of it fifty two foots in length
and forty one foots in breadth."*   It was probably remembered
by many aged people who have gone to rest within a few years,
as it stood until the early part of this century. Mr. Frederick
Fowler, now living, remembers it and the fire that destroyed it.
The bell, which was afterward procured, is said to have hung at
the centre of the roof, and to have been rung by one standing in
the middle of the ground floor. It was purchased in 1728 of
Jacob Windel, in Boston, for one hundred acres of land in the
south part of the town. Before it was procured the people were
called together by a more primitive method, as is indicated by
the following statement:

" The selectmen have agreed with Nath. Ponder to sweep the
meeting house the year ensuing and have promised him thirty
five shillings for said service, and with John Negro to beat
yᵉ drum on the Sabbath days and others as ocation may serve,
and have promised him twenty three shillings for said service,

and the first drum is to be beat against the Widow Moseleys house in good weather."

It is uncertain whether or not we are to infer from the last clause that they were habitually "fair weather christians." The building was paid for by the town, and a committee was appointed to assign sittings according to their dignity, those near the pulpit being considered most honorable, a custom that prevailed as long as the building stood.

The arrangement for Mr. Taylor's support was always liberal. His salary was at first £50, raised in 1678 to £70, and in 1686 to £80 ; in addition to which he had a generous allowance of land both in, and outside of, the settlement. The people seem also to have been considerate of his wants in many ways. In 1692, whether from bad crops or some other cause, the people seem to have felt poorer than usual, for they voted him £80, with the desire that he would abate £10 thereof. The estimation in which he was held is indicated in various ways. He was consulted in all matters relating to the temporal and spiritual interests of the church ; as, for instance, it was voted to consult with him and see whether he were willing that some timber from the old meeting-house should be used in the new one.

Early in 1722 he began to show signs of advancing age, being then eighty-one years old ; and Deacon Noble* and Capt. Ashley were appointed " to go and discourse with" him concerning the selection of a colleague. " At the same meeting Dea. Th. Noble was chosen as a messenger to go in the towns behalf to give Mr. Brown " (of New Haven) "a call, and also voated to give Th. Ashley five or six shillings to encourage him to go and accompany Deacon Noble in his journey." Mr. Brown did not come, and the following year Mr. Isaac Stiles, who had been teaching here, received and declined a call. He was Mr. Taylor's son-in-law, and his son afterward became President of Yale College.

This must have been a rather trying time for the people in church affairs ;—their minister failing in health, their efforts to secure an assistant proving unsuccessful, and their new house of worship being uncompleted. They tried for several months to make an arrangement with Mr. Bull, who was teaching here, and " Nehemiah Loomis, John Root and Jonathan Ashley were

---

*See Appendix I.

3

chosen to go and stir up the meeting house comitey to see that the meeting house be finished speedily." The next year, 1726, a house and lot were provided for the new minister, and " it was voted that the town will give Mr. Bull £50 for a year ensuing for preaching one half day each Sabbath, and to rise proportionally according to his preaching;" a vote, as has been said, of rather doubtful construction. Finally, in May, 1726, a committee was appointed to see whether Mr. Taylor " would lay down preaching." In September following, a committee was appointed to arrange for Mr. Bull's ordination at the town's charge.

I cannot ascertain whether the venerable pastor continued to preach occasionally afterward, but it is probable that he did; for the people, among whom he had labored for more than half a century, would have been glad to see him in his accustomed place and hear his familiar voice. He never fully recovered from a severe fit of sickness that prostrated him a few years before his death, which occurred June 24th, 1729, in his eighty-seventh year, after he had served this church, before and after its organization, nearly fifty-seven years. His is an enviable record, and he has transmitted to a large number of descendants, some of whom still hold land here that he owned, his unimpeachable character. There is said to have never been a scoundrel among them. Three of his daughters married ministers. Anna was the wife of the Rev. Benjamin Lord, D. D., of Norwich, Ct. ; Naomi, of the Rev. Ebenezer Devotion of Suffield, Ct. ; and Keziah, of the Rev. Isaac Stiles of North Haven, Ct. He was buried in the old cemetery, where his tombstone may still be seen, bearing the following quaint but expressive epitaph :

" Here rests the body of ye Rev'd Mr Edward Taylor ye aged, Venerable, Learned & Pious Pastor of ye church of Christ in this town, who after he had served God & his generation faithfully for many years fell asleep June 24 1729 in ye 87 year of his age."*

The events of this first pastorate have been thus explicitly detailed because it is in many respects the most remarkable of the church's history. They were days of anxiety and hardship, but also of labors cheerfully undertaken and sacrifices patiently endured. The foundations were then being laid for a structure

---

*See Appendix C.

that has honored the Divine Architect and its human builders. Had those early settlers proved indifferent to the interests of Christ's kingdom, while seeking to build homes and establish a town, subsequent generations would not have had the reason they now have to rise up and call them blessed, and we would not have had such a record of successful work for God as we now review.

As has been intimated already, efforts were made several years before Mr. Taylor's death to secure a colleague. In the latter part of 1724 the church sent to Mr. Nehemiah Bull, who had been teaching on Long Island, to serve them in that capacity. According to his own record in the church book, he first preached here on the 17th of January, 1725, from the text—I. Corinthians, viii., 4—"For there is none other God but one." For a year and a half he assisted Mr. Taylor and taught school. Negotiations with him having been finally concluded, he was ordained October 26th, 1726, one hundred and fifty-three years ago this month. Six churches were invited to take part in the Council, the three in Springfield, and those from Hatfield, Enfield, and Suffield, respectively.

Mr. Bull has left a detailed account of the exercises. All the ministers and delegates came on the evening preceding the day appointed, as was customary in those times of primitive methods of traveling, except Mr. Devotion of Suffield :

" And being gathered together it was thought by them a good thing to do what business they could that night y^t they might not be hindered next day and thereupon they thought convenient to examine into what opposition there was (for there had been as the ordination drew on a great stir) therefore they sent for the principal man who was so confident y^t he could have a great party on his side if there was a Town-meeting if the elders desired there might be a Town-meeting next morning And the Town were asked if they desired y^t Mr Bull should be ordained or that the ordination should go on that day to vote for it and the vote was so clear y^t ye Rev. Elders judged y^t the barr was clearly taken out of the way, wherefore they proceeded to solemnize that affair and those that managed the work were the Rev. Mr. Taylor &c in this order viz. The Rev. Mr. D. Brewer began the solemnities with prayer, the Rev. Mr. W. Williams preacht and then they proceeded to set me apart by laying on of hands the Rev. Mr. E. Taylor, Mr. T. Woodbridge and Mr. W. Williams laying on hands and then the Rev. Mr. T. Wood-

bridge made the first prayer and gave charge & then the Rev.
Mr. W. Williams made the last prayer and then the Rev. Mr. E.
Devotion did that which stood in the room of the right hand of
fellowship and they were done. I was directed to name a Psalm
to be sung after w^h I was (according to the custom in these
parts) directed to bless the congregation in the Father Son and
Holy Ghost and so the solemnities were finished."

Soon after this event, and before the death of Mr. Taylor, evidence is given in the church record that the beginnings of that
movement which resulted in what has been known as the Half-
Way Covenant, and so seriously disturbed the churches of New
England, were felt here ; and Mr. Bull had become securely
enough established to take the lead in presenting to the church
the following questions :

" 1. Whether such persons as come to enter into full communion may not be left at their liberty as to the giving the chh.
an account of the work of saving conversion i. e., whether Relations shall not be looked upon as a matter of indifferency, and
the chh desired some time of consideration, so the matter was
deferred till the next Lord's Day, when it was voted in the affirmative. 2. Whether a confession of faith drawn up in shorter and
more general terms should be used instead of the Assembly's
Catechism. 3. Whether all Baptized Persons who were come to
years of understanding and were capable of discipline belonging
to this congregation should be lookt upon subjects of discipline,
and voted in the affirmative. 4. Whether 5 men should not be
chosen by the chh to meet and consult with me about the issuing
cases of difficulty upon immergent occasions, this voted in the
affirmative."

Thus, in 1728, we have the first mention of what corresponds
with our church committee. Fifty years later, more definite action
was taken to secure greater efficiency of discipline. The new
confession of faith that was adopted was explicit enough as a
matter of intellectual belief, but contains no reference to personal
regeneration ; and while much longer than it, is in this respect
far more objectionable than the Half-Way Covenant of the First
Church of Springfield.*

During the pastorate of Mr. Bull, some of his flock became
hostile to him, and carried their opposition far enough to threaten
a serious breach in the church. The town passed a mild vote to
the effect that there was cause of grievance against him ; but

---

*See Appendix F.

what it was, is stated neither there nor in the church record. The latter gives an extended account of the wise and christian way in which the difficulty was finally settled. He met the people in a church meeting, that continued two afternoons and nearly a whole night; and, after friendly conference, they arrived at "an accommodation," and voted that all complaints against him should be dismissed. This was not entirely satisfactory to the disaffected ones, who shortly afterward raised a tumult and absented themselves from the sacrament. Having again called the church together, he gave a quotation from "Hooker on Church Discipline," to the effect that "men may complain of y^r Elders if y^y consider 'mselves wrong^d, but (says he) if ye complaint prove unjust and unreasonable be it at ye peril of him that complains, for he is to be censur^d sharply & severely." Mr. Bull then added a fearful scriptural example: "We all know how dreadfully God testified his anger against Corah Dathan & Abiram for complaining & murmuring against Moses and Aaron & raising a tumult against them without any sufficient cause, & there is great Reason why a due testimony sho^d be born all groundless Assaults made against ye ministers of Christ, because such things tend to wound and destroy their good names, &c." He was, perhaps, somewhat improvident; for the town record shows that, though his salary was steadily increased, yet he fell into financial embarrassments, as indicated by the following action: "November, 1735, £150 voted for salary; February 5, 1736, £125 voted to pay his debts." In 1738 and the year following, his salary was £240. His pastorate was cut short by death, April 14th, 1740, in the thirty-ninth year of his age, and the fourteenth year of his ministry. His family afterward moved to Sheffield, where his oldest son became a respected physician.*

Mr. David Parsons preached a short time as supply; and in August, 1740, four months after Mr. Bull's death, the Rev. John Ballantine was called to fill his place. The provision for his support is shown by the record. The house of the former pastor was to be bought for £700, of which a £500 interest was to be offered Mr. Ballantine to encourage him to settle.

"Also voted to give Mr. John Ballantine £200 in bills of credit of the old tenor or £200 in silver money at 28s and

---

*See Appendix E.

4d per ounce as the bills now go and his firewood for his sallary from year to year annually as long as the said Mr. Ballantine carries on the work of the ministry with us."

This is the first time a particular sum was agreed upon for more than one year. Mr. Ballantine was a native of Boston, and descended from Scotch ancestors. He was graduated in 1735 at Harvard. The vote to call him to this church was passed unanimously, after a season of "solemn fasting & prayer," and his letter of acceptance shows that he took a spiritual view of the work before him, and was deeply impressed by its responsibilities. The Committee selected to sign the letters missive, inviting neighboring churches to the Council that should ordain him, consisted of Deacon John Shepard, Capt. John Gunne and Thomas Ingersole, Esq., and each letter contained the following request: " You are desired to meet at the house of Lieut. Ashley, at nine of the clock in the morning." The Council was called for the 17th day of June, 1741 ; and before that time, answers having been received from two churches in Boston, declining their invitations, four churches in addition to those originally agreed upon were invited. This irregular proceeding, together with a difficulty in regard to the First Church of Springfield, came very near preventing the Council from performing its work. Mr. Breck, the fourth pastor at Springfield, had been ordained a few years before in the face of opposition, on account of grave suspicions cherished by some of the brethren that he was not strictly orthodox, and some of the ministry would not consent to sit in council with him and his church. The Council finally consisted of only three churches, Sunderland, Brimfield, and Springfield First. Mr. Breck made the opening prayer ; Mr. Rand preached and gave the charge ; Mr. Bridgham prayed and gave the right hand of fellowship ; they sang the one hundredth Psalm, and were dismissed with a blessing.

The year of his ordination seems to have been a very prosperous one for the church, sixty-nine members having been received on confession of faith ; a number unequaled in any previous year, and in any succeeding one until 1819, when one hundred and twenty-seven were received. The other years in our church history made memorable on account of large accessions, are 1842 and 1843, when one hundred and fifteen were added, and 1850, when the additions numbered sixty.

Mr. Ballantine seems to have been a man well suited to his place as pastor in a small town, keeping track of all matters of interest to the people, and exercising a kind of fatherly supervision over their affairs. For many years he kept a journal, in which were noted the results of his observation of current events relating to himself, his family, the church, the town, and the nation. The original manuscripts were fortunately discovered, after moulding in some obscure corner for more than half a century, and are now preserved, with other old documents of local interest, in that useful and beneficent local institution, the Atheneum. Extracts from them were published in successive numbers of the "Westfield Journal," in 1834, which show not only much of the man's character, but also give an interesting view of town life in those remote days. They are well worthy of perusal by any who have a taste for local antiquities. As they furnish about the only material from which to gain an idea of his life and ministry, I shall make such selections from them as seem most interesting on various subjects.*

During his ministry the church suffered much annoyance and perplexity by the action of the Separatists, who were a small body that withdrew from the services on account of grievances occasioned by the "half-way covenant." Some of them seem to have been sincere reformers, who were outraged by the reception of persons who did not give satisfactory evidence of regeneration, by the authority granted to the regular ministry, and by the method of taxing all citizens for the support of the church, whether or not they attended its services. About this nucleus of sincere and evangelical protesters against abuses, there gathered many others, tinctured with all sorts of wild notions, holding divers absurd religious views. Mr. Ballantine was firmly convinced of the error of their ways ; for, though the church charitably decided to consider such of their number as joined them simply no longer members of the church, instead of formally and publicly excommunicating them, yet he considered it wrong for the faithful ones who remained to run after them, as shown by the following entry :

" May 2nd, 1775. A query was proposed by a member of the church to day occasioned by one of our members attending the

---

*See Appendix G.

separate meeting last Sabbath, whether it was not disorderly to attend a meeting of Separates. It was observed that we are to mark those that cause divisions and avoid them and that since the church had withdrawn communion from the preacher it seemed absurd to receive one as a teacher whom we cannot fellowship as a brother."

Yet he was extremely liberal toward all whom he considered true christians. Having attended a meeting at Agawam, where "the pedobaptists & anti-pedobaptists brought forward terms of coalescence previously prepared," he says :

"It was a rare instance of Catholicism. I was well pleased with it. It appears to me quite reasonable that we should hold communion with those with whom we hope to live in heaven though they differ with us in some non-essentials, as the subjects & mode of baptism. All true christians are members of Christ ; if one of the members of our body should be imagined by us to be out of order, or should be really so, should we neglect it, or cast it away? should we not try to recover it? or if we had no hopes of that we should make ourselves easy with it. So should christians deal with each other. It is arrogance in any man to set himself up as the standard & condemn or approve others according as they appear when measured by this standard. I disclaim infallibility in myself, and will not allow it in others."

He was either in advance of his church at this time in liberality, or else they backslid from the high ground then occupied ; for, in 1788, twenty-seven years later, they refused to grant the request of Anna Phelps for a letter to the Baptist Church.

The plainness of his preaching, and his patience under injuries, are illustrated by the following entries : "I was insulted to-day by a principal man in town for a plain sermon delivered last Sabbath against idleness. May none of these things move me ; may I not be left to render reviling for reviling ;"—with more in the same strain.

"May 20th, 1762. Married David Mosely. I asked none of the guests though the wedding was at my house. I preferred not to do much. Esq. Mosely made a supper and judged it better to invite the guests himself. May 24. Some pretend that we not only did not invite them but hindered their being invited to the wedding. What need of prudence has a minister ! It is a most seasonable caution, 'Be ye wise as serpents & harmless as doves.' "

His heart was pained by the decline of religion in his day, though we are apt to think the old times were so much better than the new. When English recruits started to attack the French in Canada, he says: " May 16, 1759. The men who were enlisted marched to-day. There used to be a sermon or prayers with them, but nothing of the nature now ; as if they had come to the conclusion that it is vain to seek God." His anxiety must have diminished soon afterward, for, on the 28th of the next month, he notes : " Fast throughout the Province to seek God's blessing on the expedition against Canada." And the public spirit of the day was sufficiently virtuous to uphold conviction and punishment for profanity ; for, in 1760 : " James Wilson sentenced to sit in the stocks for profane swearing paid his fine." He did not hesitate to reprove popular sins, though lightly considered by offenders : " In consequence of finding in the contribution box the other day a pewter dollar and some other pewter coins I preached from Acts 5 : 1-11,"—which is the account of Ananias and Sapphira.

Some of his comments are exceedingly pithy and bright, as note the following : " Aug. 17, 1762. Many law suits, the consequence of extravagance, imprudence, idleness, fraud & covetousness." " June 31, 1766. Attended the funeral of Deliverance Hanchett, aged 72. She was never married, maintained by the town, unhappy in her temper, provoking in her language, lived undesired, & died unlamented." This is perhaps more truthful than many epitaphs of the time ; though " the truth is not always to be spoken."

Mr. Ballantine must have been able to perform an immense amount of work ; for, on a day when detained from church by sickness, he says : " Have not been kept away but one day and a half for twenty years." The Rev. Mr. Atwater, his successor, had an experience almost as remarkable in this respect. In twenty years he was prevented from preaching one Sunday on account of illness, and two Sundays because of lameness. It was not then, as now, necessary for ministers to spend three months of the year in Europe to recuperate their wasted energies.

During the latter part of Mr. Ballantine's term of service, a long-continued case of discipline perplexed the church. It was finally suggested to call a mutual council, but each party wanted the other to bear its expense. Neither yielding, it was proposed

4

that, if the offending brother should be adjudged guilty by the council, he should pay the cost; but, if he should be acquitted, the church should pay it. The matter was finally compromised by each agreeing to pay one-half. Seven churches met, and spent three days trying to effect harmony; but their work was done in vain, since he was afterward debarred from the Lord's table.

Mr. Ballantine died February 12th, 1776, aged sixty, after having served the church faithfully for thirty-five years. In the " Hampden Pulpit," compiled by the Rev. Dr. Davis, it is stated that three of his sons received a collegiate education; that one of them, Ebenezer, became a physician, and was the father of Rev. Henry Ballantine, missionary to India, and Rev. Elisha, Professor in Union Theological Seminary in Virginia, and afterwards pastor of a church in the city of Washington.* The Rev. John Ashley was called after Mr. Ballantine's death, but was not settled.

The Rev. Noah Atwater was called from the position of Tutor in Yale College, (which he had held three years,) after preaching here as a supply; and, after some hesitancy, accepted, and was ordained November 21st, 1781. He was a student of more than ordinary ability, as is evidenced by the fact that he was graduated from Yale College with the first honors of his class of 1774. After a pastorate of twenty years, he died quite suddenly, his twentieth anniversary sermon having been the last he ever preached. It was published at the town expense, together with his funeral sermon delivered by Dr. Lathrop, who was pastor of the church at West Springfield sixty-five years. A copy (probably the only one now in existence) of the two sermons has been kindly loaned me for perusal by his grandson, Mr. William L. Atwater, of New York. Dr. Lathrop gives quite an extensive sketch of him. He says:

" He was blessed with superior abilities, a clear understanding, a capacious mind, and a solid judgement. He loved good men whatever name they might bear. He was a wise and pacific counsellor in the churches and studied the things which made for peace among his own people. He was remarkably tender of character, inclined to speak well of all when he could, and cautious not to speak evil of any but when he ought. His

---

*See Appendix G.

discourses were replete with sentiment, composed with perspicuity & adapted to the promotion of godliness. His prayers were solemn and devout, and his delivery was grave and commanding. Whatever he spoke appeared to come from a feeling heart and it reached the heart which could feel. He had many friends & I believe no enemies. If he had enemies, either they did not know him or did not love good men. There were none whom he treated as enemies or seemed to suspect as such. In a word his ministerial life was a useful pattern to his brethren, and his christian life was an instructive copy to his people."

He was interested in practical science, kept a rain gauge and thermometer, and received a premium for an essay on the cankerworm.

Did time permit, I would be glad to give a synopsis of, and extracts from, his last sermon already referred to. The title page, as published, reads as follows : " A sermon on the preservation and changes of human life, by Rev. Noah Atwater A. M., late Pastor of the church at Westfield, delivered to his people on the 22nd of November 1801 at the close of the 20th year of his ministry and under a distressing and threatening disorder of body, which soon after terminated his life." The text is Acts xxvi., 22 :—" Having therefore obtained help of God, I continue unto this day." The same words from which Dr. Davis preached on the last Sunday of his life. He states that there were then in the town two thousand one hundred and eighty-five souls, and continues : " When I was ordained the number of communicants was 135. Of these, two thirds are gone from us ; 70, more than one half, are dead, and 20 have removed to other places ; but 45 remain." He received into the church one hundred and twenty-one members. During the first year of his ministry he visited every family in town, and during the twentieth he almost repeated the task. His advice to his only son, printed with the sermons, shows shrewd observation of men and things, great practical wisdom, sound sense, and ardent piety. In places it is not unworthy of Polonius, in the well-known parting advice to Laertes. I cannot forbear giving a few of its most striking injunctions :

" Be above little things & despise them wherever they appear. Be as frugal in your expenses as you can consistently with a decent reputation. Learn the art of being esteemed manly and generous by spending but a little. Always speak and

walk and act naturally. Be always wise, kind, mild, and conde-
scending; and yet keep at a proper distance from all improper
intimacies."

As a token of the estimation in which Mr. Atwater was held,
we have the town's action, voting that his family should have
free use of the parsonage and ministry land for one year after
his death, and that a printed copy of his last sermon should be
given to each family in town.

The first evidence of a movement to secure another meeting-
house appears on the record of the town under date of April 6th,
1801, when a committee of seventeen was chosen, one from each
school district, to select a site for it. As on previous occasions,
there was considerable controversy respecting it. Part of the
people even thought it expedient to enlarge the building then
occupied; an idea that was earnestly supported during the following two years, till the edifice was burned to the ground, as has
always been supposed, at the instigation of the opposing party;
but, though the town offered a reward of $300 for the conviction
of the incendiary, he was never discovered. The crowded condition of the old building is indicated by the fact that, while it
contained thirty-three pews on the ground floor, most of which
were six feet square, capable of seating fifteen persons each, or
altogether four hundred and ninety-five, the last official seating
provided for six hundred and fifty adults, many of whom were
heads of families. The report of the seating committee of that
year, the original of which is preserved at the Atheneum, con-
cludes as follows:

" Your Committee would farther observe, that they find it im-
possible to accommodate the inhabitants with seats in the Pews
of the House should they all attend meeting they would therefore recommend that precedence or priority cannot, nor ought
not to take place, by reason of any one being named or read off
as first in any Pew, but that all have equal right to a seat in the
Pews to which they are assign'd indiscriminately, & that a Spirit
of accommodation only can alleviate the embarrassment & be a
substitute for our present cram'd situation & condition.
                              WILLIAM SHEPHARD, per order."

The new meeting-house was located, after considerable discus-
sion, where the present building stands, on ground bought by the
town for $236. Most of the pews were sold in advance, thereby

realizing the sum of $6,019 as a building fund, with which, in consideration of a right to fifteen pews, the town agreed to finish it and keep it in repair. It was decided by town vote to have two flights of stairs leading up to the pulpit, and subsequently, that they should be winding, in case any one could be found who would pay the difference in cost between that and the straight form. Some people afterward brought into town-meeting a grievance based on the needless sacrifice of space and obstruction to view of the double flight. An ornamental pillar from the front of the old pulpit is on exhibition here to-day. The pew next the pulpit stairs was assigned to the use of the minister forever. The building was dedicated January 1st, 1806, the Rev. Mr. Knapp preaching the sermon; and it was used nearly fifty-five years, then sold for $1000, and moved back, where it still stands, to make way for the present structure. During the time of its use one thousand one hundred and eighty-eight members were received into the church, while during the previous one hundred and twenty-seven years the number reached only nine hundred and fifty-seven.

The first mention of special sacramental utensils for use of the church, is a statement in its record, that "about the year 1785, Mr. Joshua Green of Boston made a present to the church of a Bason to be used at Baptism and the church voted their thanks to him for his kindness." Mr. Atwater afterward left $20 by will to furnish the table, and the church voted to raise an equal sum by subscription; but the Hon. Samuel Fowler rendered that effort unnecessary by a gift, indicated in an accompanying note as follows: "I with pleasure herewith present to the church in this town two silver plated Flagons (the first cost in London being forty-five dollars) which I hope will be acceptable to the church." These were received with thanks, and his name was engraven on them, with the date of presentation. They are here for inspection to-day. In 1824, the church received by will from the same generous donor, two more flagons and a baptismal basin, the former of which are still in use at communion seasons. After the erection of the marble font by an unknown friend some years ago, the basin was presented to Plymouth Congregational Church of Minneapolis, Minn.

The Rev. Isaac Knapp was ordained to the ministry in this church November 16th, 1803. He was a graduate of Williams

College in the class of 1800, and served there two years as Tutor before settling here. He died in 1847, in the seventy-fourth year of his age, and the forty-fourth year of his pastorate. After 1835, because of failing health, he was able to preach but little, and was assisted by a colleague.

Though distinctly remembered by many now living, little documentary material available for a biographical sketch remains. Dr. Davis, in the "Hampden Pulpit," characterizes him as " a man of uncommon prudence, of great kindness of disposition, conservative, sound in faith, and who lived agreeable to his profession." He was exceedingly affable, scrupulous for the finer points of etiquette, courtly in his manners. He is said to have bowed always three times on meeting an acquaintance. His pastorate was marked by peace and harmony among his own people, and he was ever ready to afford wise counsel for the settlement of any disputes brought to him for arbitration. Mr. Bates, in the town bi-centennial address, says: " He knew the wants of his people ; he appreciated the interests of the community ; and few men were more ready to afford more valuable suggestions."

During the latter years of Mr. Knapp's active service, two trifling innovations, one in the service of the church, the other relating to the comfort of the worshipers, disturbed some of the people. About 1820 small sums began to be paid for sacred music ; and in 1824 the town voted $75 for sacred music, "to be assessed on Mr. Knapp's salary." If this means, as it seems to, that it was to be deducted therefrom, it must have been an expensive luxury for him, however the people may have enjoyed it, since his salary was only a little above $400, although larger than when first settled. The people had become so accustomed to long pastorates that, when he came, they " voted to add £15 to £100 voted as salary to Mr. Knapp, to commence five years from ordination." The other innovation was in heating the meeting-house. In December, 1823, the matter was brought up in town-meeting, when it was decided not to procure stoves and window-blinds, but a committee was appointed to ascertain the cost of the former. For four winters more the people shivered through the services ; but in December, 1827, it was voted, " that the selectmen procure at the expense of the Congregational Society of this town, two stoves together with the pipes not to exceed in amount $80."

Here I would gladly conclude this discourse, and resume it at another time, in order to have a better opportunity than is now afforded to do justice to the life-work among you of the Rev. Emerson Davis, D. D. My only consolation is in the fact that the memories of so many of you are well stored with facts respecting him, tenderly and gratefully cherished. No one can become thoroughly acquainted with the present life of this church and this town without recognizing the broad and deep results of his long and faithful ministry. His life here was the out-working of a principle which he selected as the subject of his valedictory oration on graduating from college : "To be useful, the duty and happiness of man." His was a useful life in the broadest sense, bringing to bear upon this community at so many points an elevating and impulsive force, which is still in operation. In the spheres of education, morals and religion, he was ever zealous and efficient; and in each of them this town owes him a debt of gratitude, which demands that many generations yet to appear should rise up and call him blessed.

It is a matter of profound satisfaction to all who knew him and have learned to honor him, that she, who was such a worthy help-meet for him, is with us to-day.

Dr. Davis was born in Ware, July 15th, 1798, and was graduated from Williams College in 1821. After having been Preceptor of the Westfield Academy for fourteen years, he was ordained as colleague of the Rev. Mr. Knapp. His theological training was received under Dr. Griffin, President of Williams, with the interests of which institution he was closely identified, serving as Tutor one year, as Trustee thirty-three years, and as Vice-President seven years.

His pastorate here was eminently successful in the best sense of the term. From its commencement, June 1st, 1836, to its close, the church had reason to thank God for it. During its earlier years it was marked by special religious interest; for many years there were additions to the church at every communion season, and no year of the long period passed, that was not marked by accessions.

The thirtieth anniversary of his settlement, on which he preached a sermon reviewing his ministry, was his last Sunday on earth. The following Friday, June 8th, 1866, sickness suddenly attacked him at teachers' meeting, and he died within a short time. President Hopkins says of him in his funeral sermon:

"His qualities of mind were not brilliant; but he was conscientious, industrious, punctual, judicious, kind, faithful; and through these qualities, he gradually won the confidence and affections of the whole community, as well as the devoted love and reverence of his people. * * * He came up in his influence imperceptibly, as one of your grand elms. No man perceived the moment of its increase; but at length it stood with its top in the heavens, and with its branches wide spread for beauty and for shade."

The only colony formally organized from this church is that which was started in 1856. A little band of sixty-three persons left their old home, bearing a parent's blessing, and were organized into a church by a council that convened May 22d of that year. They soon afterward erected the commodious and handsome building in which they still worship, at a cost of about $25,000; to which a convenient chapel has since been added. The child has grown to vigorous and stalwart maturity, and now stands and works side by side with the parent. Organized in a true missionary spirit to meet the growing needs of the town, the Second Church has always lived on terms of the utmost harmony with those in the old household; the utmost kindness and affection mark all their relations with each other, and they cordially unite to carry on the common work of the Lord. After having been served one year by the Rev. Francis Homes, the church settled the Rev. J. S. Bingham as its first pastor in 1857, who was followed, after six years of labor, by the Rev. George Bowler. He was succeeded in June, 1866, by the Rev. Henry Hopkins, whose able and faithful service has been rendered ever since with a tenderness and kindness of heart that have won for him affectionate and grateful friends throughout the community. It is hoped that he will so far imbibe the spirit of the old church as to follow the example of her long line of ministers who considered their settlement a life tenure.

The house of worship which the young organization soon erected, incited the people of the old society to build this structure, at an expense of about $25,000. It was dedicated in 1860, and, I understand, is practically free from indebtedness.

The Rev. E. H. Richardson succeeded Dr. Davis in the pastorate after a year had intervened, and was installed May 1st, 1867, coming here from Providence, R. I. He accepted a call to Hartford, Ct., in 1872, and is now in New Britain, of that state. He was followed by the Rev. A. J. Titsworth, called from the Seminary in 1873, who resigned in 1878, to accept the pastorate of the First Church at Chelsea.

The departure of these two respected and beloved pastors, who had labored earnestly and efficiently, after five years of service, occasioned the people great grief and disappointment; and the expressions of mutual regret and regard that were called forth by the separation, show that both they and the people suffered from it.

It is a remarkable fact in these days of short pastorates and unsettled supplies, that the first six pastors of this church began and ended their ministerial work here, and were laid to rest by their grateful and loving people. Their average term of service is thirty-two years.

Your present pastor was called from Brooklyn, N. Y., and installed May 14th of the current year, beginning the third century of the church's history as its ninth pastor.

The church has been served by thirty deacons, among whom are four Deweys, three Fowlers, three Roots, two Ashleys, three Shepards, two Searles, and two Smiths.

Gen. William Shepard, who has secured an honored place in history through his heroic services in the French and Indian and Revolutionary wars, a friend of Washington and Lafayette, after laying aside his sword, was chosen to the office in 1789, and served twenty-eight years, till his death in 1817, aged eighty. He was one of the most remarkable men ever connected with this church. A copy of the sermon preached at his funeral by Mr. Knapp, is carefully preserved by his great-granddaughter, one of our members, and an extended sketch of his character and career is given in the town bi-centennial address.

The whole number of members who have been connected with this church from its foundation till now, if my count of their names on the church record be correct, is two thousand five hundred and seventy-six, received as follows: By Mr. Taylor, two hundred and thirty-one; by Mr. Bull, two hundred and twenty; by Mr. Ballantine, four hundred and twenty-two; by Mr. Atwater, one hundred and twenty-one; by Mr. Knapp, six hun-

5

dred and seventy; by Dr. Davis, six hundred and fifty-one; by
Mr. Richardson, one hundred and thirty-nine; by Mr. Titsworth,
one hundred and eight; by others, fourteen. They would make
a vast company could all be gathered together.

The early history of the Sunday-school is not preserved in any
existing records; but at least two of the scholars first collected
still live among us, Mrs. Samuel Horton and Mrs. Frederick
Fowler. The latter remembers quite clearly her experience in
that capacity, and has in possession an "Evangelical Primer,"
containing several catechisms, given her for good behavior, and
a book of quaint hymns for children. Both these, with the Bible,
were studied by the scholars. The school is supposed to have
been organized in the spring of 1817, and met in the old Academy Hall for several years. An invitation to act as teachers,
addressed to Mr. Zabina Fowler, afterward a deacon, and Miss
Nancy, his sister, signed by six directors, is still preserved by
one of our people. Mrs. Fowler remembers a visit to the school
of Dr. Osgood, of Springfield, who spoke of the work of Robert
Raikes in England. The superintendents, so far as I can learn,
have consisted of the following brethren, in about the order in
which they are here given: Deacons Stearns and Stowe, Mr.
Chapman, Deacons Chadwick and Smith, Dr. Goodrich, Mr.
Greenough, Rev. Mr. Titsworth, Mr. Todd, and Deacon Frank
P. Searle, the present incumbent.

It will doubtless be interesting to know what are the localities
of historic interest to this church, and they should be kept clearly
in memory. The first meeting-house stood a few rods northwest
of the west end of the iron bridge that now crosses Little River,
on land afterward used for the town pound, and now owned by
Mr. William Todd. The second building stood on the corner of
Main and Meadow streets, in what is now Mr. George H. Mosley's
garden. The road, now Meadow street, forked, and ran on the
east and west side of it. The third house occupied the site of
the building we are in, which is the fourth provided by the
church. Mr. Taylor lived not far from his meeting-house, on a
road running north, a short distance west of it, and died in his
son's house, an old red one, that stood till a few years ago on
the corner made by the road just mentioned and Main street.
Mr. Bull and Mr. Ballantine lived on the south side of Main
street, on land running west from the corner of what is now

Cross street, on land since owned by the late Mr. Caleb Fowler, whose first wife was Mr. Ballantine's granddaughter. Mr. Atwater's house was just west of where the Atheneum now stands. Mr. Knapp's house, since moved to another site, stood just west of Mr. E. R. Van Deusen's house on Franklin street. Dr. Davis lived on Elm street, just north of Arnold, about where Loomis's hardware store now stands. The First and Second Churches each built a commodious and comfortable parsonage several years since. The first four pastors were buried in the old burying-ground, and Mr. Knapp and Dr. Davis in the Pine Hill cemetery. A tablet was placed in the church in memory of Mr. Taylor by Homer and Henry T. Morgan, of New York, two of his descendants, and one to the memory of Dr. Davis was placed here by his people.

The support of the ministry of this church has been partly provided for by sundry gifts to a ministerial fund, amounting now to about $6,500 in the hands of trustees.* It has been derived in part by sale of the ministry land, and in part by legacies; the first of which, in the church books, is that of Samuel Root, probably a son of the third deacon of the church. His will was drawn in 1711.

Many other details of historic interest might be added to this sketch did time permit, but your patience was long since overtaxed.

Two hundred years of the church's life are gone beyond our power to recall or influence them. The lessons learned by reviewing them are to be applied to present duties, through whose performance the future may be affected. With devout gratitude for God's mercies, so bountifully vouchsafed during all these years, let us determine to be more faithful in requiting them; and in glad recognition of the christian usefulness of generations that have been gathered to their fathers, let us follow in their steps, as they have followed Christ; ever lifting heavenward, from zealous hearts, loyal to Him and loyal to this our beloved church, the prayer suggesting that Fast Day sermon two hundred years ago: "The Lord be with us as He was with our Fathers."

*See Appendix H.

Appendix.

A.

The copy of the letter missive, inviting the five churches of Norwich, Windsor,. Springfield, Northampton and Hadley to the council that organized the church here, is partly illegible, through the ravages of time. As an interesting historical document, it is herewith given as fully as possible :

"Hon^rd & Rev^nd S^r : together with ye Much Respected chh of Christ at Norwich in which you serve.

After ye manifold Temptations & experienced Difficulties of one nature & another that we ye Professed servants of Christ in this place have met withall, & been delayed thereby, with respect unto ye Interest of Christ in a Gospell instituted Order : it hath graciously pleased ye Divine Omnipresent Preserver, ye father of Spirits & ye God of all Mercy in Christ, so far to shine forth upon us, as to lead us by ye hand, so, through ye same as to bring us to a conclusion among o'selves to fix upon ye last fourth day of ye sixth month next ensuing, for ye managem^nt of that solemn & holy work of entrance into a city fframe, a chh Instituted State. And thereupon in sense of our own Insufflsionsie for it, need of Advice, Directions & Assistance, as also ye Right Hand of Fellowship in, & about ye same : as also considering ye Result of civill Authority in this matter, y^t it behooveth us as o^r Master to fulfill all Righteousness : & also the custom of the chh of Christ (wch in all commendable things is greatly to be adhered unto) harmonizing herein, we have fixt on certain churches to request them to allow unto us their Aide, Help & ffellowship in this business * * * * also desire that you would accept of such a burden of Christ in ye Gospell put upon you by us in this desire, as y^t you would send y^r Rev^nd Elders & Messengers to help & incourage us in this worke y^t is to be carried on by us upon ye day above mentioned.

Thus earnestly desiring ye Everlasting ffather, ye Prince of Peace & ye Eternall Spirit of love that sitts between ye Cherubims, y^t is in ye midst of ye Golden Candlesticks & y^t speakes unto ye churches, to prevent all impediments, obstructions to oᵉ motion, to stir you up to all readiness of mind to accept thereof: to give his gratious presence to you, & by & with you unto us, we remaine, subscribing oᵉselves

Yᵉ Neighbors ffriends, Companions & Brethren in yᵉ common Interest of Christ

| WESTFIELD July 1679 | { EDWARD TAYLOR
JOHN MAUDESLEY
ENSIGN SAMᴸ LOOMIS } | { SER. DEWY
ISAAK PHELPS
JOHN ROOT } |

These for yᵉ Revⁿᵈ. Mr. J. F. pastor of, together with yᵉ chh of Christ at Norwich."

B.

In his sketch of the first Council, Mr. Taylor records the formal commission from the authorities of the Colony for the task of organizing the church :

" ☞ I then gave an account of the work of the day and inquired into the order of our motions hitherto and our liberty for the same from

{ Civill Authority
{ Church dismission of members.

As for the answer unto the first this following order which was granted the foregoing year was presented and read. August 9ᵗʰ, 1678.

These doe signifie that we approve yᵉ christian people in yᵉ colony of Massachusetts to enter into a church state according to yᵉ rules of Christ and yᵉ laws of yᵉ country in that case provided and in particular the persons hereunder named viz. Mr. Edward Taylor minister, John Maudesly, Samuel Loomis, Isaak Phelps, Thomas Gun, Josiah Dewy and John Root, who have made application to us, who together with such others living in that place whom God hath fitted as living stones for that spiritual building (having testimony of their professed subjection unto yᵉ gospell of Christ) we do allow to enter church state and commend them to yᵉ Lord's gracious blessing. Signed yᵉ day and year above written. JOHN LEVERETT, Govʳ.

SIMEON BROADSTREET DANIEL GOODWIN SR THOMAS DANFORTH JOHN PYNCHON EDWARD TING JOSEPH DUDLY	Assist.

Thomas Gun, John Maudesley, Samuel Loomis and Isaak Phelps were recommended by letters " writ to myself," as Mr.

Taylor says, from Windsor. John Root brought a letter from Farmington, Josiah Dewy and John Ingerson from Northampton.

C.

From a letter received by the Hon. William G. Bates at the time of celebrating the town bi-centennial, from Mr. Henry W. Taylor, of Canandaigua, N. Y., a few brief extracts may properly be made to heighten our estimate and enlarge our conception of the first pastor. The whole sketch, as given in the Bi-Centennial volume, is well worthy of perusal:

" He was born in England, educated for the ministry, studied seven years in one of their universities; but the ejection of two thousand dissenting clergymen in 1662, and the persecutions which that class of christians suffered, induced him to a voluntary exile. He was, through his whole life, a most voluminous writer, keeping a diary of the running events of his life, and recording things of passing interest. He left a large number of written folio volumes, and he was in the habit of transcribing, with his own hand, the books which were loaned to him by his friend Judge Sewall of Boston. * * * Mr. Taylor also studied medicine; and during his life was accustomed to minister as well to the diseases of the body, as of the soul. He also gave attention to natural history, and some of his compositions were published in the scientific literature of the day."

The writer of the above, his great-grandson, has a small book of his, inscribed on the title-page:

"Such things as are herein contained are the Principalls of Physick, as to the practical part thereof, being extracts of that famous Physician, Riverius."

In the same book President Stiles, Mr. Edward Taylor's grandson, bears witness to his attainments as a literary man:

"He was an excellent classical scholar, being master of the three learned languages, a great historian, and every way a very learned man. He was an incessant student, but used no spectacle glasses to his death. I have a manuscript folio of six hundred pages, his commentary upon the Evangelists. * * * * A man of small stature, but firm; of quick passions, yet serious and grave."

A MODEL LOVE LETTER.

The following is a copy of the original letter among the collections in the Connecticut Historical Society, written by the Rev. Edward Taylor, of Westfield, Massachusetts, July, 1674, to Miss Elizabeth Fitch, daughter of the Rev. James Fitch, one of the original proprietors, and the first clergyman settled in the town of Norwich.

This letter was written by the Rev. Mr. Taylor to Miss Fitch —reputed to have been a beautiful and accomplished lady— during his courtship, and was to have been read, if opportunity offered, at the bi-centennial dinner, by Colonel George L. Perkins, a great-great-grandson of the Rev. Mr. Fitch :

WESTFIELD, Mass., 8th day of the 7th month, 1674.

My Dove :—I send you not my heart, for that I hope is sent to Heaven long since, and unless it has awfully deceived me it hath not taken up its lodgings in any one's bosom on this side the royal city of the Great King ; but yet the most of it that is allowed to be layed out upon any creature doth safely and singly fall to your share. So much my post pigeon presents you with here in these lines. Look not (I entreat you) on it as one of love's hyperboles. If I borrow the beams of some sparkling metaphor to illustrate my respects unto thyself by, for you having made my breast the cabinet of your affections as I yours mine, I know not how to offer a fitter comparison to set out my love by, than to compare it unto a golden ball of pure fire rolling up and down my breast, from which there flies now and then a spark like a glorious beam from the body of the flaming sun. But alas ! striving to catch these sparks into a love letter unto yourself, and to gild it with them as with a sun beam, find, that by what time they have fallen through my pen upon my paper, they have lost their shine and fall only like a little smoke thereon instead of gilding them. Wherefore, finding myself so much deceived, I am ready to begrudge my instruments, for though my love within my breast is so large that my heart is not sufficient to contain it, yet they can make it no more room to ride into, than to squeeze it up betwixt my black ink and white paper. But know that it is the coarsest part that is couchant there, for the finest is too fine to clothe in any linguist and huswifry, or to be expressed in words, and though this letter bears but the coarsest part to you, yet the purest is improved for you. But now, my dear love, lest my letter should be judged the lavish language of a lover's pen, I shall endeavor to show that conjugal love ought to exceed all other love. 1st, appears from that which it represents, viz. : The respect there is betwixt Christ and his church, Eph. 5th, 25th, although it differs from that in kind ; for that is spiritual and this human, and in degree, that is boundless and transcendent, this limited and subordinate ; yet it holds out that this should be cordial and with respect to all other transcendent. 2d, Because conjugal love is the ground of conjugal union, or conjugal sharing the effects of this love. is also a ground of this union. 3d, From those Christian duties which are incumbent on persons in this state as not only a serving God together, a praying together, a joining in the ruling and instructing their family together, which could not be carried on as it should be without a great degree of true love, and also a mutual giving each other to each other, a mutual succoring each other in all states, ails, grievances ; and how can this be when there is not a love exceeding all other love to any creature? And hereby if persons in this state have not love exceeding all love, it's with them for the most part as with the strings of an instrument not tuned up, when struck upon makes but a jarring, harsh sound. But when we get the wires of an instrument equally drawn up, and rightly struck upon, sound together, make sweet music whose harmony doth enravish the ear ; so when the golden strings of true affection are struck up into a right conjugal love, thus sweetly doth this state then harmonize to the comfort of each other and to the glory of God when sanctified. But yet, the conjugal love must exceed all other, yet it must be kept within bounds, for it must be subordinate to God's glory ; the which that mine may be so, it having got you in its heart, doth offer my heart with you in it as a more rich sacrifice into God through Christ, and so it subscribeth me,

Your true love till death,

EDWARD TAYLOR.

This for my friend and only beloved
Miss Elizabeth Fitch,
at her father's house in Norwich.

The reader of this letter does not fully appreciate it, and can not do so, without seeing the *fac-simile* of it. An imperfect description can not do justice to it. The reverend gentleman brought the fine arts to his aid ; and rightly so, for love itself is one of the fine arts, and is so denominated by one of the old Roman poets.

Our types do not allow us to copy the pictorial illustrations ; but our readers may fancy a " pen and ink sketch " of what he calls a dove, in the lower corner of the letter, of the size of an old-fashioned ninepence, without feathers, and looking like a plucked chicken. It was necessary to denude it of its feathers,

6

to have room to inscribe upon the side of its body the following couplet:

> This dove and olive branch to you
> Is both a post and emblem too.

INVENTORY OF REV. EDWARD TAYLOR.

IN RECORDS OF PROBATE OFFICE OF NORTHAMPTON, VOL. 5.—AN ANCIENT TOME BOUND IN HOG-SKIN PARCHMENT.

Hampshire Westfield, Oct. 14th, 1729 Deacon David Ashley & James Dewey & Nehemiah Loomis were appointed & sworn to apprize the estate of the Rev^d Mr. Edward Taylor Lately Deceased in Westfield afores^d. John Ashley Just. Peace. An Inventory of the Estate of the Revnd. Mr. Edward Taylor Deceased this done Aug. 29th, 1729

MR. EDW^D TAYLOR.

No. 1.—A Great coat 20s. A lined Jacket 20s. A shirt 6s, a shirt 3s, a pair of breeches 2s. Two pair of breeches 1s. A Hat 13s. Gloves 1s. 2 Bands 1s. 6d. An old Gown 3s. A Jacket 3s. Two brown under Jackets 2s. A white woolen under Jacket 6d. To a Bed and Bolster in the Parlour Chamber £3. 15 : 0. A set of brown stamped brown curtains & Valliants 15s. Bedsted Rope & Rods 20s. Hair Cloth 20s. An old flower'd Rug at 5s. A white Blanket at 8s. A Good Flower'd Rug at 25s. A white Rug 10s. A Flag Matt, 1s. 6d. A Streaked Pillow 5s. A Red Rug 5s. An old Feather Bed in the Parlour 40s. A Bolster 9s. A Pillow 6s. A Blanket with black streaks 6s. A Set of Red Curtains & Valliants 30s. An old under Bed 2s. Bedstead & Rop. 20s. A new Bed in the outward chamber £3. An underbed 2s. another old underbed 3s. Old streaked curtains Valle^{ce} & Bedstead 6s. An old Bolster some feathers in it 3s. A Bed in the outw^d room Bolster & Pillows £4. 15s. Two Rugs in the outward room 30s. the Bedstead Ropes & Matt. 5s. An old white Blanket 3s. An old piece of Green Broad Cloth 3s. A pair of sheets 18s. A good sheet 9s. 3 old sheets 11s. A sheet 8s. An old sheet 3s. Two sheets 20s. Two old sheets 3s. An old sheet 2s. 6d. An old Cotten sheet 4s. A good sheet 8s. Another good sheet 8s. A pair of Good sheets 25s. Six Cotten Napkins 18s. An old Holland Table cloth 3s. Another Table Cloth 2s. 5 Towells wove with a wale 7s. 6d. Two old Towells 1s. Two Towells 2s. A Holland Pillow Bier 3s. 2 Pillow biers 2s. 6d. A Table Cloth 1s. 6d. A Napkin 1s. A strainer 1s. A Great Pie Plate 10s. A Great Platter 14s. A Platter 13s. Another Platter 13s. 3 Platters 36s. 3 more Platters 30s. One Platter 10s. one Platter 12s. two Platters 18s. A little Platter 3s. 5 plates 15s. Two old plates 4s. A Bason 4s. 6d. 2 basons 4s. 6d. 2 little basons 2s. 6d. A pint cup, 4s. 6d. Old Pewter 6s. A

Tankard 6s. 6d. Part & wheels 10s. Cups & Tin 2s. 6d. A Coller 6s.

No. 2.—Traces 18s. A Slead 6s. Small Caps & pin 2s. 1 Hoe 5s. An ax 4s. 2 Wedges 4s. Beetle rings 2s 6d. Yoak & Irons 5s. Several Old Rings & pieces of fetters 3s. An ax 6s. Another pail 2s. Another pail 1s. 2 pottles 2s. A churn 2s. 6d. Dishes & Trenchers 3s. A Great wheel 5s. A little wheel 5s. A wreal 2s. 6d. A cheese fat & straining dish 1s. 6d. An ol l Book 1s. Cards 2s. 6d. Old Iron 2s. 2 old Barrels 3s. Scales & Waits 1s. 6d. Knives & forks 6s. A pair of shears & 2 little bottles 1s. 6d. A Sow & two pigs 36s. Another sow 30s. 9 swarms of bees £4. 10s. 0d. Two forks 3s. A Plow & Irons 20s. Plow chain 14s. A Rug in the Garret 15s. A hammer 1s. 6d. A Heifer £3. 5s. 0d. A little heifer 17s. Another heifer £1. 14s. 0d. A Young horse £7. 0s. 0d. A Colt 50s. A Malt Trough 10s.

No. 3.—A Great Kettle £5. 0s. 0d. A Midling Kettle £2. 15s. 0d. A Less Kettle, £1. 15s. 0d. A little Skillit 6s. A Three leged Brass pan 18s. A Brass Pan 20s. A Great Skillit 10s. A Pie pan 4s. A brass Scummer & Ladle 7s. 6d. A Brass Candlestick 4s. A flat candlestick 2s. Hand Irons Brass Plates 16s. Hand Iron Tops 8s. A warming Pan 25s. An Iron Dish Kettle 17s. An Iron Pot 20s. one Trammel 6s. Another Trammel 4s. Pothooks 3s. A pair of Tongs 6s. Another pair 4s. A slice 4s. Great Hand Irons 20s. Grid Irons 12s. Great Flat Hand Irons 6s. Little Slim Hand Irons, 4s. Grid Iron 5s. frying pan 9s. A spit 5s. A Brass Chopping Dish & little piece of Bass 4s. A Burning Iron 1s. A Fender 1s. A Branding Iron 2s. A turn Gouge 1s. A Swivle 1s. 6d. A Box Iron & Heaters 6s. An Iron Candlestick 1s. Hetchels 5s. Musket 10 s. A Pistol 4s. A Hewing Ax 2s. 6d. A Parcel of old Iron 2s. 6d. Collerhooks 1s. A Plain Iron 6s. hammer 1s. A chamber pot 1s. A Tunnel 10d. paper box 4d. A Paper Morter & Pestle 3s. 6d. Earthen Pans 1s. 4d. Great Table in ye Parlour 25s. A Great Table in the Outwd Room 20s. A Silver Tankard £15. 5s. 0d. A two ear'd cup, one Pottinger a salt seller & 4 spoons & a drain cup Total wt. 37 oz. £34 : 0s. 0d. A Black Cow £5. 10s. 0d. The Gallows cow £5. 10. 0d. The Lined Cow £5. 5s. 0d. A little Table 8s. 5 chairs 15s. 3 chairs 7s. 6d. 2 Great chairs 6s. one 2. Two high chairs 7s. 2 Old chairs 1s. A Chest of Drawers 30s. A Narrow chest 2s. 6d. A long form 7s. A Cuphoard Cushion 10s. A Looking Glass 2s. A stall 1s. 6d. A chair table 11s. A Looking Glass 16s. A carved chest 16s. A new chest 6s. A Trunk 6s. An Indian bark 1s. A little square trunk 1s. A joint stool 3s. A compass 1s. A flaskit 5s. The Studdy Table 10s. The little old bellows 4s. An old hour glass 1s. A Box in the Studdy 4s. Wooden Steelyards 1s. 2 old chests 5s. A

Half bush[ll] 2s. 6d.   A two pound weight 1s.   3 Sievs 1s. 6d.   2
old barrels 2s.   A Pork barrel 2s. 6d.   A Cider barrel 2s.   A
cider barrel 3s.   A small Cask 1s. 6d.   A Beer barrel 2s.   A
Powdering Tub 2s.   2 old Casks in the Celler 2s.   An old lye tub
1s.   A Mashing Tub, 2s.   A half tub 1s.   Funnel 2s.

The total valuation of his property thus inventoried amounts
to £182, 0s., 6d. That of his library, which is also inventoried
in the same record, is £54, 4s., 7d.

D.

After receiving the impressive deliverance of Samuell Partridge, who was Judge of Probate of Hampshire County, respecting the site of the second meeting-house, it was voted that his report should be the " finall ishew " of the matter.

" At the same meeting it was voated by the town that they
would begin to raise the new meeting house on Wednesday morning at 2 hours by sun in the morning the 8th day of this instant
June, assembling to work at the beat of drum every morning
until it is over.

At the same meeting it was voated y[t] all men belonging to the
town shall assist in the work of raising the meeting house from
17 years of age & upwards on pain & penalty of 3 shillings pr.
day for every days neglect duering the time of raising ex all
such as shall make a satisfactory excuse to the Comitey y[t] have
the chairge of y[e] mater.

At the same meeting it was voated that the comitey shall have
liberty to prepare four or five barels of beer at the town charge
for that consern above mentioned.

At the same meeting it was voated that Captain Phelps,
Deacon Noble & ·Deacon Ashley should go & desier Mr. Taylor
to come to the place of raising the meeting house then & their at
the time appointed to seek to God for his guide & protection in
the work of raising."

E.

The Rev. Nehemiah Bull was descended from an ancient and
honorable family of that name in Hartford. His great-grand-
father, Capt. Thomas Bull, one of the early settlers of that city,
was honorably and usefully connected with the bloody battle

against the Pequot Indians in May, 1637, when, as a historian of the period has said:

" More bravery was displayed and greater good achieved to New England, than by any battle which has since been fought, not excepting the battle of Bunker Hill. The Pequots were the most warlike and blood-thirsty Indian nation in New England. By this action they were defeated and ruined as a nation, as their fort was destroyed, seventy wigwams burned, about six hundred Indians killed in the action by fire and sword, with only about seventy active white men in the field ; by which action Connecticut was saved."

Rev. Mr. Bull's oldest son, William, a physician, married Jane, daughter of Colonel John Ashley, of Sheffield. They had a son William, who entered the profession of his father.

F.

The " Half-Way Covenant," to which reference has been made, is here given in full :

" I believe (we) y^t there is one only living & true God Infinite Eternal & Unchangeable in his being, wisdom, Power, Holiness, Justice, Goodness & Truth, Distinguished into & subsisting in 3 Persons, who are ye same in substance essence & attributes Equal in Authority, Glory & Majesty but distinguished by their —— & personal propertys, ye father being ye first in order begetting ye Son, ye Son ye 2^d begotten of ye father, ye Holy Ghost ye 3^d proceeding from ye father & ye Son. I (we) believe y^t this God is ye Almighty Creator ye wise & Good upholder, ye Just Sovereign Governour & disposer of all his creatures & all their actions. I (we) believe y^t man created in his image in a state of integrity was placed under a covenant of life upon condition of perfect obedience but by his disobedience lost both his uprightness & title to life & is by nature in a state of weakness enmity, pollution, Guilt, unrighteousness & wrath. I (we) believe y^t when ye fullness of time was come God sent forth his only begotten Son to take upon him ye nature of man y^t so subsisting in 2 distinct natures (divine & human in one Person) he might be a fit Mediator between God & man suitably qualified to Redeem man by price & power & effectively Reconcile him to God, for which end God appointed (gave permission to) his Son, to be a Prophet, Priest & King to his church, who did in ye days of his flesh execute these offices by obeying ye Law, Revealing ye Gospell & suffering death, & when he had continued under ye power of death for a time he arose from ye dead, ascended into heaven & sat down on ye Right hand of God where he now continues to execute ye several offices of a Mediator, Pleading his own merits on ye behalf of ye elect, interceding for em, sending ye Holy Sp^t to inlighten, convince, effectually call & sanctify those that are given to him, who being innabled to believe in his name to ye justification of their persons shall be openly acquitted, pronounced blessed & invited by ye Supreme judge to take possession of ye Kingdom of glory prepared for em, at that day when God shall weigh y^e —— both just & unjust, & shall judge ye herets of men by J : Christ who also will condemn all that obey not ye gospel to everlasting punishm^t according to ye scriptures of wrath wch I believe to be ye word of God & ye only rule of faith & manners."

G.

The wife of Mr. Ballantine was Mary Gay, niece of the Rev. Ebenezer Gay, who was pastor of the First Church at Hingham for sixty-nine years; called by Savage, "the honored patriarch of the New England pulpit of that age." The excellent traits and remarkable talents of Mrs. Ballantine are matters of tradition.

The intellectual gifts of the Gay family have descended to her posterity, some of whom have been lights to the heathen in foreign lands. The interesting work recently published, entitled, "Midnight Marches through Persia," was written by one of her descendants. A book in our own Sunday-school library, showing how desirable it is to be "shod with peace," was written by another descendant, residing here.

Lydia Gay, a niece of Mrs. Ballantine, rode to Westfield from Dedham on a pillion behind the parson. She came to be an inmate of his family, and married Col. David Mosely, a great-grandson of John Maudesley, one of the "foundation-men." She lived to the age of ninety-four years, a gentle and lovable old lady; who, as she sat and knit at that remarkable age, entertained her great-grandchildren with many reminiscences of Mr. Ballantine's family. To one of them I am indebted for these facts.

The following additional citations from Mr. Ballantine's diary, quoted from in the sermon, are not without interest :

"Jan. 21st, 1764. Attended the funeral of Nath. Pynchon at Springfield, whom I fitted for college. They gave me and my wife a pair of gloves."

This seems to have been his first observation of a custom that has continued to some extent to the present day, at least so far as to provide the officiating clergyman with them.

"Jan. 17, 1768. I preached. Sang twice in the forenoon. The singers stood up in the gallery and sang new tunes. Some disgusted and left the house."

Nearly twenty years before this, according to the church record, "it was proposed that Dr. Watts' version of the Psalms should be used at the administration of the Lord's Supper. No objections." But the new-fangled tunes seem to have caused righteous indignation in those who had courage to express it.

Mr. Ballantine took special pains to record what was unusual, mysterious, or grotesque, as the following entries indicate :

"Went to Granville. In the night the house of Mr. Jonathan Rose took fire and was consumed. Mr. R. was burnt in it, a man 90 years old. All the remains of the body might have been put in a half-peck measure."

"Attended Capt. Clapp's funeral. As they were letting the coffin down, the head string broke ; it fell and broke off the lid and split the head ; it was taken up and mended."

(Query.—Does the last clause refer to the coffin or the head?)

The following is suggestive of the generous doses of medicine prescribed to patients before the disciples of Hahnemann discovered the efficacy of sugar pellets : Mr. Israel Noble was sick of a fever, and Dr. Pynchon of Springfield having been called, thought the case hopeless, "but prescribed rhubarb, liquorice, cream of tartar and some other smaller matters, together with a decoction of the Cortex (P. bark) and claret wine, pap of wheat bread and rice." Surely, if not hopeless before, it must have been after taking such a remedy ! He goes on to say, showing the prevalence of superstition in that day : "Mr. Noble and wife heard last fall an unusual knocking at the door, which began about daybreak and continued till sunrise. They could hear no voice, nor see any one, though they got up." Perhaps it was an ominous premonition of the Doctor's knock.

One more entry is added, illustrative of the generosity of his people, and the sentiment of the times on what is now a subject of practical morality : On the eve of his daughter's wedding, October 16th, 1768, the following articles were sent to the parsonage, which would be hardly duplicated now, degenerate as the times are :

"Mrs. Parks, 1 gallon of rum. Capt. Mosely, 2 qts. Dea. Shepard, a leg of mutton. ' Mrs. Clapp, 1 qt. rum. Thos. Root. 2 qts. of brandy. Matt. Noble, flour and suet. Ensign Noble, some butter. Clark King, pig. Ensign Ingersoll, 2 qts. rum. Mrs. Ashley, a loyn of mutton and butter. Mrs. Kellogg, some cranberries. David Mosely, a pig and 3 fowls. N. Weller, a piece of veal and suet. Ensign Weller, apples. Mrs. Ford, cabbage and potatoes. S. Noble, 2 fowls. D. Root, 2 qts. brandy."

Reference is made in the sermon to two grandsons of Mr. Ballantine who entered the ministry. The six children of Henry, who was missionary in India, are now in that country ; one son a minister, another a physician, the three daughters are wives of missionaries—Mrs. Harding, Mrs. Fairbanks, and Mrs. Parks. Two sons of Elisha are ministers. Henry W. is at Bloomfield, N. J., and William Gay is Professor in Ripon College, Wisconsin. Henry and Elisha were sons of a physician, but he had a brother, William Gay, who was a clergyman. Thus the ministry has secured representatives from four successive generations of that family.

H.

Through the courtesy of Dr. H. W. Clapp, of this town, I have been allowed to see a copy of the will of one of his remote ancestors, which provides for what was probably the first legacy ever made for the support of the ministry in Westfield. The donor was Capt. Roger Clapp, who was a very remarkable man. From 1665 to 1686 he was the redoubtable commander of the Castle in Boston Harbor, now Fort Independence. He would not permit a soldier to serve under him who was not a professing christian. He died in 1691, at a good old age, leaving in his will the following clause :

" I giue out of my farme at pachasack in westfield fifty acors

unto the inhabitance of that towne towards the maintenance of
· an able minister in that towne with this prowiso: that they paye
or cause to be pay two busshels of good wheat unto my dear wife
in boston yearly during her naturall life."

I.

Deacon Thomas Noble, of whom mention is made in the sermon, was the second of the name in the church. Thomas Noble,
Sr., his father, was one of the early settlers of Springfield, reach-
ing there in 1653. He moved to Westfield probably in the
autumn of 1668, and immediately became prominent in town
affairs, serving in various responsible positions. He was for a
time constable, and afterward county surveyor. The Hampshire
County records indicate that he once got into difficulty for not
obeying the stringent laws of the time respecting the observance
of Fast Day:

"At a County Corte held at Northampton, March 27th, 1683.
Thomas Noble of Westfield being p'sented by the Grand jury for
Travelling on a day of Humiliation, publiquely appointed by the
Genll Corte, which he owned, pleading his necessity for Comeing
home, and yet this Corte Considering said offense, being a grow-
ing evil amongst us, many Persons too much disregarding such
Extraordinary Dutys & Seasons, have adjudged sd. Noble to pay
as a fine to the County treasurer five shillings."

Mr. Noble was the emigrant ancestor of the largest family
bearing the name in the United States.

7

J.

1679.   BI-CENTENNIAL   1879.

OF THE

First Congregational Church

OF

WESTFIELD, MASS.

To ....

You are invited to attend the Bi-Centennial Celebration of the First Congregational Church of Westfield, on

SUNDAY, October 5, 1879,

Consisting of a Memorial Sermon by the Pastor at the morning service, and a Service of Praise in the evening.

A copy of the Sermon, when published, will be sent you gratuitously on the receipt of a request for it.

Yours in behalf of the Committee,

HERBERT LYMAN.

Westfield, Mass., September 17, 1879.

Responses to Letters of Invitation.

MRS. E. WILLIAMS, Fall River, Mass.
MR. & MRS. J. D. TAYLOR, Minneapolis, Minn.
MISS HATTIE C. MERWIN, Vinton, Ia.
FRED. KING, Austin, Minn.
S. MUNSON, Albany, N. Y.
MRS. LEWIS PARSONS, Northampton, Mass.
J. FOWLER, Castalia, O.
MRS. GEORGE B. CLARK, Cambridgeport. Mass.
MRS. TURNER S. CLEVELAND, Salem, N. Y.
CHARLES HUTCHINS, Boston. Mass.
MRS. C. W. FARNAM, Brooklyn, Cal.
SELAH MERRILL, Andover, Mass.
G. C. LANDON, Frenchtown. N. J.
JOHN M. BALLANTINE, Taunton, Mass.
M S. HUERD, Wilbraham, Mass.
MRS. ROBERT WHITNEY, Peterboro, N. H.
REV. E. J. HURLBUT, Mittineague, Mass.
REV. A. J. TITSWORTH. Chelsea, Mass.
MRS. A. S. HALE, Minneapolis, Minn.
L. C. SHEPARD, Menasha, Wis.
J. B. ELDREDGE, Hartford. Conn.
D. S. ROWE. Tarrytown, N. Y.
J. C. ATWATER, New York City.
D. A. FITCH, Strawn, Kan.
MRS. C. W. SHEPARD, Litchfield, Conn.
REV. B. M. FULLERTON, Palmer, Mass.

JOS. W. KING, Jacksonville, Ill.
SAMUEL C. LEWIS, Tarrytown, N. Y.
MRS. D. W. INGERSOLL, Constantia, N. Y.
EDWARD TAYLOR, Andover, Mass.
REV. DANIEL BUTLER. Waverly, Mass.
JOHN EDMANS, Philadelphia. Pa.
H. E. SIMMONS, New York City.
WM. L. ATWATER, New York City.
H. T. MORGAN, New York City.
M. T. GLEASON, Newton, Mass.
GEO. E. KNAPP, Bloomington. Ill.
HIRAM SMITH, Hillsdale, Mich.
REV. L. D. CALKINS, West Springfield.
DANIEL MUNSON, Binghamton, N. Y.
MRS. IRA G. WHITNEY, New York City.
ROLAND MATHER, Hartford, Conn.
MARTIN N. DAY, New York City.
A. P. CARY, Gloucester, Mass.
MISS E. C HALLIDAY, Brooklyn, N. Y.
MISS NANCY MARSH, Providence, R. I.
MRS. H. B. STOCKWELL, Providence, R. I.
G. MUNSON, Huntington, Mass.
W. B. C. PEARSONS. Holyoke, Mass.
SAMUEL A. GREEN, Boston, Mass.
REV. S. G. BUCKINGHAM, Springfield, Mass.
REV. W. GLADDEN, Springfield. Mass.
MRS. G. W. CAMPBELL, Pittsfield, Mass.
REV. WM. E. DICKINSON, Chicopee, Mass.
A. T. EDSON, Feeding Hills, Mass.

[*From The Western Hampden Times and News-Letter of Oct. 8, 1879.*]

THE FIRST CHURCH OF WESTFIELD.

CELEBRATES ITS TWO-HUNDREDTH ANNIVERSARY.—REV. J. H. LOCK-
WOOD'S SERMON IN FULL.

A large assembly gathered at the First Church last Sabbath
morning to listen to the services commemorating the two-hundredth anniversary of the Society's natal day. The church
was tastefully and elaborately decorated with flowers and evergreens, handsomely and artistically arranged in bouquets, festoons, garlands, and other exquisite formations and impressive
devices. Shields, bearing the names of the eight "foundation-
men" of the church, were arranged along the front of the gal-
leries, four on each side of the house, hung between festoons of
evergreens, and decorated with flowers, cereals, and "the full
corn in the ear." The tablets of Rev. Edward Taylor and Rev.
Dr. Davis were appropriately garlanded, the one with leaves of
the oak, and the other with roses ;—the latter speaking of a later
bereavement, though both equally proclaiming that "the memory
of the just is blessed." An arch built over the pulpit bore on its
crest the dates "1679—1879," while a scroll winding gracefully
around the two pillars, intertwined with leaf and flower, bore the
names of the eight pastors of the church who preceded Mr. Lockwood. Portraits of the pastors of the Second Church were prettily
grouped and decorated on the front of the west gallery. Two
large autumn bouquets, placed in front of Mr. Lockwood's desk,
were universally admired for the artistic combination of their
colors and the harmonious blending of their soft autumnal tints.
Great praise is due to George Houghton, carpenter, and R. T.
King, artist, for executing so faithfully and efficiently the chaste
and elegant designs of the committee of ladies and gentlemen
who had the matter in charge. To say that the ladies deserve a
share of credit for the meritorious display would be almost su-
perfluous ; their taste and judgment and skill were discernible in
it all.

A quartette, composed of Mrs. Mary Mullen, Miss Mary E.
Kingsley, H. B. Stevens, Esq., and Prof. Le Clair of Holyoke,
began the exercises by singing Kotzschman's "Te Deum, in F."
Rev. Henry Hopkins read passages from Scripture appropriate

to the occasion, and offered prayer. Singing by the congregation of "All hail the power of Jesus' name," followed. After which, Rev. Mr. Lockwood delivered an able and comprehensive historical discourse, which we give to our readers in full. Though a comparative stranger to our town, it can be said, with as much surprise as justice, that Mr. Lockwood, by diligent study and hard work among the musty records of the last two centuries, not only did complete justice to the occasion historically, but he caught the inspiration of the hour, and seemed to stand, and to make his hearers stand, in the august and almost divine presence of his great and venerated predecessors as he graphically unrolled the history of the First Church of Westfield for the last two hundred years. For lack of time, Mr. Lockwood could not use all the wealth of antique lore that he had mined for the occasion ; but we are requested to announce that the pamphlet edition of the sermon, soon to be issued, will contain, in an ample appendix, much of the deferred material.

A praise service in the evening worthily closed the anniversary exercises. Several fine selections were well rendered by the quartette of the morning, assisted by Mrs. R. W. Parks and Miss Mattie Loomis ; selections of Scripture were read by Rev. Mr. Lockwood ; and a brief, but able, discourse, eulogistic of the First Church and its founders, was given by Rev. Mr. Hopkins. Congregational singing also added to the enjoyment of the occasion. Mr. Hopkins spoke of the impressiveness of the occasion and of the tender and persuasive influences of the hour, calling all to cast in their lot with the people of God. After expressing the obligation of the churches to Mr. Lockwood, for the patient research and exacting toil which the writing of his sermon had demanded, he said :

"It is proper for me to thank you especially for your kind mention of us in the Second Church, and also to recognize gratefully the cordial christian courtesy of our reception here to-day. In the name of the church, I most heartily assure you that we join you in the wish—and we will make the wish an endeavor—that the same harmony which has characterized the past may continue always. Next to the spiritual growth and power of our own, we desire that of this one, that stands side by side and shoulder to shoulder with her. It is perfectly certain that any thing which injures one hurts the other, and that any thing that gives new life to the one is a blessing to the other. The circumstances attending the separation in 1856 were calculated to produce a spirit of true fellowship. We went out because the old home was crowded. Some one must go, and you gave us your blessing. Dr. Davis counseled and carried out the colonization. His two sermons, entitled, ' Church Extension,' published at the request of the Second Church and Society, are a true setting forth of the whole case. The first sermon was preached the Sabbath before the commencement of public worship by the colony in Music Hall, and the second on the occasion of the organizing of the church. There was no quarreling about it, no party strife, no schism in the body of Christ. It was only organizing another regiment in the same holy service. That movement, so inaugurated, was not a mistake. God has blessed it. Of the sixty members who, many of them with tears, cut loose from the old organization, thirty-three are still members of the Second Church. These are here with hearts aglow to-day. They are like naturalized citizens of our Republic, to whom every thing in the national life and history in the fatherland belongs fully up to the time of the new relation, and who, in the new-found ties, do not forget to feel love and pride for the old. But the fact is, we all feel so. Just as American citizens have a right to share in all the glory and renown of old England on land and on sea, in every great name in her literature or war, statesmanship or philanthropy, up to July 4th, 1776, so we lay claim to the old church history as a part of our heritage, and to every revered and honored name, down to May, 1856."

Mr. Hopkins briefly sketched the original settlement, by the site of the iron bridge, with its fort over a cellar and its two miles of palisades, as pictured by Mr. Bates in his bi-centennial address, and called attention to the fact recorded by him, that, in 1677, the General Court provided for " the consolidation of the people into a more compact community," and that then, as appears from the records of Massachusetts, " the proprietors of town lots in Westfield near their ' meeting house,'" made certain agreements. They had, then, in 1677, before the organization of their church, "a meeting house," provision for the worship of God, and for the church that was to be. This seems to answer the question asked in the sermon as to the original church building, and reveals the fact that, at the very start, central in the settlement, as essential a part of it as the fort or the dwellings, stood the house of God. Were those brave, hard-worked men and women right in this thing? Yes, thank God, they were right. They had little thought of symbolism in religion ; but in this they unconsciously made use of a true symbolism. The rude church stood central among their rude homes, as the religious principle is central in man, and as it must be made central in every enduring form of society. The love of God's house, not of the rough log building " thirty-six feet square," not of the house made with hands, but of that living temple, the church of God, was characterized as the deep, tender, life-giving, divine principle that dwelt in the fathers. This, more than their rigid, puritanic sense of duty, was that which distinguishes them. This has been the potential, the moulding influence that has come down from them. They put first that which is first forever more. They made central in their hearts and homes and in their common life, that which in all rightly-organized life is central forever more. The lesson of all this history is a plain one, not to be forgotten by us. Those whom we commemorate honored the church of God ; and God honored them according to His everlasting ordinance and in the fulfillment of His faithful promise.

On Monday evening, the ladies prepared a banquet in the church parlors, which was appreciatingly indulged in by both churches—progenitor and offspring.

THUS ENDETH THE SECOND CENTURY.

PRAISE SERVICE

AT

The First Congregational Church,

WESTFIELD, MASS.,

SUNDAY EVENING, OCTOBER 5, 1879,

In Commemoration of the Two-Hundredth Anniversary of its Foundation.

ORDER OF SERVICE.

I. ORGAN VOLUNTARY.

II. OLD HUNDRED. (*Congregation.*)
"Be Thou, O God, exalted high."

III. INVOCATION.

IV. ANTHEM: "Let the people praise Thee." (*Choir.*)
From Costa's "Eli."

V. SCRIPTURE SENTENCES.

VI. AMSTERDAM. (*Congregation.*)
"Rise, my soul, and stretch thy wings."

VII. SCRIPTURE: Deut., 26 Chap.

VIII. ARIEL. (*Congregation.*)
"O could I speak the matchless worth."

IX. PRAYER, (closing with Lord's Prayer, in concert.)

X. ANTHEM: "Jerusalem, my glorious home." (*Choir.*)

XI. ANTHEM: Denmark. (*Congregation.*)
"Before Jehovah's awful throne."

XII. ADDRESS, BY REV. HENRY HOPKINS.

XIII. ANTHEM: "How lovely are the Messengers." (*Choir.*)
From Mendelssohn's "St. Paul."

XIV. LYONS. (*Congregation.*)
"Ye servants of God, your Master proclaim."

XV. SCRIPTURE: Ps. 95 and 96.

XVI. LENOX. (*Congregation.*)
"Ye boundless realms of joy."

XVII. ANTHEM: "Praise be unto God." (*Choir.*)
From Spohr's "Last Judgment."

XVIII. PRAYER.

XIX. SHINING SHORE. (*Congregation*)
"My days are gliding swiftly by."

XX. BENEDICTION.

www.ingramcontent.com/pod-product-compliance
Lightning Source LLC
Chambersburg PA
CBHW031759090426
42739CB00008B/1086